Serenity

THE SCHOOL OF LIFE
Essential Ideas

Serenity

Published in 2024 by The School of Life
First published in the USA in 2024
930 High Road, London, N12 9RT

Copyright © The School of Life 2024

Designed and typeset by Myfanwy Vernon-Hunt
Printed in China by Leo Paper Group

A proportion of this book has appeared online at
www.theschooloflife.com/articles

Every effort has been made to contact the copyright holders
of the material reproduced in this book. If any have been
inadvertently overlooked, the publisher will be pleased to
make restitution at the earliest opportunity.

The School of Life publishes a range of books on essential topics
in psychological and emotional life, including relationships,
parenting, friendship, careers and fulfilment. The aim is always
to help us to understand ourselves better – and thereby to
grow calmer, less confused and more purposeful. Discover
our full range of titles, including books for children, here:
www.theschooloflife.com/books

The School of Life also offers a comprehensive therapy service,
which complements, and draws upon, our published works:
www.theschooloflife.com/therapy

www.theschooloflife.com

ISBN 978-1-916753-26-6

10 9 8 7 6 5 4 3 2 1

Contents

Introduction

Nowadays, almost all of us wish we could be calmer. It's one of the distinctive longings of the modern age. Across history, people have tended to seek out adventure and excitement. But the desire to be more tranquil and focused is the new, ever more urgent priority.

We face unprecedented difficulties in holding on to anything serene or soothing. We are continually – with the help of monstrous technologies – being goaded towards fury, excitement, panic and distraction. No hour of the day is free of reminders of where else we should be, what else we need to do.

We don't keep a close eye on the true price of our noisy lives; we don't properly add up what the trip to another country on business might have done to our levels of serenity and creativity or to our relationship with those who matter. We don't notice how agitated every newspaper article makes us feel and how dispiriting every encounter with a false friend can prove. We don't understand that insomnia is our minds' revenge for all the thoughts we have carefully managed not to have in the day and our anxiety is a bid for us to pay heed to our neglected sensitivity.

What follows is 25 ideas on serenity that help us to understand the sources of our anxiety and frustrations and guide us towards the more peaceful life we crave.

A Quiet Life

A quiet life sounds like an option that only the defeated would ever be inclined to praise. The age is overwhelmingly alive to the benefits of active, social, complex and ambitious ways of living. Lauding a quiet life has some of the eccentricity of praising rain.

We are suspicious because the defenders of quiet lives have so often come from the most implausible sections of the community – slackers, hippies, the work-shy, the fired – those who seem like they never had a choice; people whose quiet lives appear to have been imposed upon them by their own ineptitude.

Yet, when we examine things further, busy lives turn out to have so many incidental costs that we have been collectively committed to ignoring. At the top, alongside our privileges, we may grow impoverished in curious ways. Our every word may be listened to with trembling respect within a vast organisation, but what we cannot do is admit that we are extremely tired and want to spend the afternoon reading on the sofa. We become strangers to those who love us outside of our wealth and status, while depending ever more on the fickle attention of those for whom we are our achievements alone. Our children see ever less of us. Our spouses grow bitter. We may own the wealth of continents, but it has been ten years at least since we last had the chance to do nothing for a day.

At this point in history, we are so fixated on the idea that poverty must always be involuntary and therefore the result of lack of talent and indigence, we have trouble imagining that it might be the result of an intelligent and skilled person's free choice based on a rational evaluation of costs and benefits. It might sincerely be possible for someone to decide not to take the better-paid job, not because they had no chance, but because, having surveyed the externalities involved, they did not think them worth it.

When we come to know the true price some ways of life exact, we may realise we are not willing to pay for the envy, fear, deceit and anxiety. Our days on earth are limited. For the sake of true riches, we may willingly, and with no loss of dignity, opt to become a little more reclusive, temperate and obscure.

Anger

We start to reduce the danger of anger through the insight that not everything that makes us sad makes us angry. We may be irritated that it is raining, but we are unlikely ever to respond to a shower by screaming. We aren't overwhelmed by anger whenever we are frustrated; we are sent into a rage only when we first allowed ourselves to believe in a hopeful scenario that was then dashed suddenly and apparently without warning. Our greatest furies spring from unfortunate events that we had not factored into our vision of reality.

We typically think of anger as a dark and pessimistic state of mind. But behind anger lies a surprising emotion: optimism. Beneath their ranting, the angry are possessed of some recklessly optimistic notions of how life might go. They are not merely in a destructive fury; they are in the grip of hope.

The person who shouts every time they encounter a traffic jam betrays a faith, at once touching and demented, that roads must always be traffic-free. The person who loses their temper with every new employee or partner evinces a curious belief that perfection is an option for the human animal.

Serenity therefore begins with pessimism. We must learn to disappoint ourselves at leisure before the world ever has a chance to slap us by surprise at a time of its own choosing. The angry must learn to check their fury via a systematic, patient surrender of their more fervent hopes. They need to be carefully inducted into the darkest realities of life, to the stupidities of others, to the ineluctable failings of technology, to the necessary flaws of infrastructure. They should start each day with a short yet thorough premeditation on the many humiliations and insults to which the coming hours risk subjecting them.

One of the goals of civilisation is to instruct us in how to be sad rather than angry. Sadness may not sound very appealing, but in this context it carries a huge advantage. It allows us to detach our emotional energies from fruitless fury around things that (however bad) we cannot change and that are the fault of no-one in particular and – after a period of mourning – to refocus our efforts in places where our few remaining hopes and expectations have a realistic chance of success.

Animals

Animals don't set out to teach us anything, but we have a lot to learn from our interactions with them, nevertheless.

Imagine that we come back from work late. It's been a tricky day: a threatened resignation, an enraged supplier, two delayed trains ... But none of the mayhem is of any concern to one friend waiting by the door, uncomplicatedly pleased to see us: Pippi, a two-year-old border terrier with an appetite for catching a deflated football in her jaws. She wants to play, even if it's past nine o'clock now, with us in the chair and her sliding around the kitchen, and, unexpectedly, so do we. We're not offended by her lack of overall interest in us; it's at the root of our delight. Here, at last, is someone indifferent to almost everything about us except for our dexterity at ball-throwing; someone who doesn't care about the Brussels meeting, who will forgive us for not warning the finance department in time about the tax rebates and for whom the conference is beyond imagining.

One of the most consoling aspects of animals – whether a dog, sheep, lizard or beetle – is that their priorities have nothing to do with our own perilous and tortured agendas. They are redemptively unconcerned with everything we are and want. They implicitly mock our self-importance and absorption and so return us to a fairer, more modest, sense of our role on the planet.

A sheep doesn't know about our feelings of jealousy; it has no interest in our humiliation and bitterness around a colleague; it has never sent an email. On a walk in the hills, it simply ambles towards the path we're on and looks curiously at us, then takes a lazy mouthful of grass, chewing from the side of its mouth as though it were gum. One of its companions approaches and sits next to it, wool to wool; for a second, they exchange what appears to be a knowing, mildly amused, glance.

Ducks nibble at the weeds, waddle down to the water and paddle about in circles without any interest in which century it happens to be from a human point of view; they've never heard of the economy; they don't know what country they live in; they don't have new ideas or regret what happened yesterday. They don't care about the career hurdles or relationship status of the person who sprinkles a few breadcrumbs near them.

Time around animals invites us into a world in which most of the things that obsess us have no significance. It corrects our characteristic over-investment in matters that make only a limited contribution to the essential task of existence: to be kind, to make the most of our talents, to love and to appreciate.

Catastrophising

The idea of a catastrophiser has an almost comedic ring to it. We picture someone sweet-but-silly running around feeling like the sky will cave in. 'There they go again,' we might say, as the catastrophiser once more insists that 'this is the end!' – while in fact, there's just a small delay with the plane, the keys have been mislaid, or it's a tickly cough.

But from close up, there is nothing remotely benign or funny about being the subject of catastrophic thinking. A mind prey to this disease can never picture any solid steps between the present and the very worst scenarios – only and always a direct line. If an ex-partner is unhappy with them, the catastrophiser won't imagine that this is only one mood of theirs, that this former lover is broadly benign and understanding. Instead, the most dire conclusion is immediate: the ex will be furious and bent on unending torture. As on so many other occasions (with the disgruntled employee or the frustrated neighbour), the catastrophiser will irresistibly reach for the most awful and pitiless story. It will be impossible to sleep, they will lose their appetite, they won't have any energy to see friends, their whole future will be called into question. There is simply no such thing as a 'small' issue.

The catastrophiser may, across most of their lives, have attained minimal insight into their way of thinking, let alone compassion for it. It seems to be just the way things are. The unfortunate catastrophiser might be on the receiving end of a great many recommendations to 'stop worrying'.

What this neglects is that catastrophic thinking is a clinical condition – and that it tends to have a history. It is almost always a symptom of having encountered a real full-blown catastrophe somewhere before. It may not be an encounter with a catastrophic *event* so much as familiarity with catastrophic *feelings* – which are generally much easier to lose sight of or to be actively disguised by those who caused them for us.

Catastrophisers have made a deduction about what will happen on the basis of what has – at some point – already happened. They might, as a toddler, have been on the receiving end of volcanic rage from a parent. The parent might not actually have excommunicated them, but that is certainly what it felt like – in that kitchen, when the crockery was smashed, and the screaming didn't let up for twenty minutes.

There is a lot of our history bound up in what we catastrophise about. A question to ask ourselves is: what bit of my past is the catastrophic scenario I fear telling me about? What does the awful thing I dread hint to me about the awful thing I have previously gone through?

We begin to get a handle on our catastrophic imaginations not by being told to be calm or learning about the theories of the ancient Stoics, but when we can develop the courage to explore what once went very wrong and then learn to distinguish then from now.

We begin to soothe ourselves by remembering that we are no longer the children we once were. We have allies, we can call professionals, we have access to law courts and hospitals. Something requires our concern; but – whatever our agitated minds so often like to tell us – it lies in the past, not the future.

Domesticity

Without our quite noticing it, and to our immense misfortune, the value of domestic life has come to occupy a degraded position in our collective vision of importance.

The pleasures and challenges of managing a household can be made to seem almost comically trivial in comparison to making a great fortune in business, succeeding in sport or entertainment, or occupying a prominent place in the media.

Yet the small, bounded, repetitive issues of the domestic realm play a great part in the essential task of living and dying well. 'If we wish to be happy, we must learn to cultivate our garden' was Voltaire's legendary and deliberately unheroic advice on the matter.

A consequence of our disregard for domesticity is that we often become enraged by what we consider 'small' irritants. Couples fall out spectacularly over whether it is necessary to use a chopping board when cutting bread, how clean the bathroom needs to be or whether it matters if a drawer is left slightly open. What fuels the conflict is a sense that these are trivial matters, unworthy of careful discussion, on which there may be varied and dignified schools of thought.

The fiendish irony is that we behave with exactly this respect around other details that matter much less in our lives. Art historians will hold an international conference on the pose of a hand in a painting by Picasso; huge corporations will devote immense efforts to finding just the right words to announce the merits of a chocolate bar to the world.

We don't always despise details; we are guided by the larger cultural picture of whether a detail deserves attention. Tragically, our culture currently assigns precious little importance to a great many details in the 'garden' of domesticity.

Early Nights

To a surprising, and almost humiliating, extent, some of the gravest problems we face during a day can be traced back to a brutally simple fact: that we have not had enough sleep the night before.

The idea sounds profoundly offensive. There are surely greater issues than tiredness. We are likely to be up against genuine hurdles: the economic situation, politics, problems at work, tensions in our relationship, the family …

These are true difficulties. But what we often fail to appreciate is the extent to which our ability to confront them with courage and resilience is dependent on a range of distinctly 'small' or 'low' factors: what our blood sugar level is like, when we last had a proper hug from someone, how much water we've drunk – and how many hours we've rested.

We tend to resist such analyses of our troubles. It can feel like an insult to our rational, adult dignity to think that our sense of gloom might stem from exhaustion. We would sooner identify ourselves as up against an existential crisis than see ourselves as sleep deprived.

We should be careful of under- but also of over-intellectualising. To be happy, we require large, serious things (money, freedom, love), but we need a lot of semi-insultingly little things too (a good diet, hugs, rest).

Anyone who has ever looked after babies knows this well. When life becomes too much for them, it is almost always because they are tired, thirsty or hungry. With this in mind, it should be no insult to insist that we never allow ourselves to adopt a truly tragic stance until we have first investigated whether we need to have some orange juice or lie down for a while.

Probably as a hangover from childhood, 'staying up late' feels a little glamorous and even exciting; late at night is when (in theory) the most fascinating things happen. But in a wiser culture than our own, some of the most revered people in the land would, on a regular basis, be shown taking to bed early. There would be competitions highlighting sensible bedtimes. We would be reminded of the pleasures of already being in bed when the last of the evening light still lingers in the sky. Our problems would not thereby disappear, but our strength to confront them would at points critically increase.

Good
Materialism

It doesn't seem to make sense to suggest that there might be such a thing as 'good materialism': after all, surely materialism is just plain bad? When people want to pinpoint the root cause of corruption in our age, they generally only need to point the finger at our attachment to material things. We're apparently sick because we're so materialistic.

It can seem as if we're faced with a stark choice. Either you can be materialistic: obsessed with money and possessions, shallow and selfish. Or you can reject materialism, be good and focus on more important matters of the spirit.

But most of us are, in our hearts, stuck somewhere between these two choices, which is uncomfortable. We are still enmeshed in the desire to possess – but we are encouraged to feel rather bad about it.

Yet, crucially, it's not actually materialism – the pure fact of buying things and getting excited by possessions – that's ever really the problem. We're failing to make a clear distinction between good and bad versions of materialism.

Let's try to understand good materialism through a slightly unusual route: religion. Because we see them as focused exclusively on spiritual things, it can be surprising to note how much use religions have made of material things. They have spent a lot of time making and thinking about temples, monasteries, artworks, clothes and ceremonies.

However, they have cared about these things for one reason only – because they have wanted material things to serve the highest and noblest purpose: the development of our souls. It is just that they have recognised that we are incarnate sensory bodily beings – and that the way to get through to our souls has to be, at least in part, through our bodies (rather than merely through the intellect).

In the Catholic Mass, great significance is accorded to bread and wine, which are believed to be transubstantiations of Christ; that is, material objects which simultaneously have a spiritual identity, just as Jesus himself combined the spiritual and the bodily while on earth.

This can sound like a very weird and arcane point entirely removed from the local shopping mall – but the same concept actually applies outside of religion. Many good material possessions can be said to involve a kind of 'transubstantiation', whereby they are both practical and physical and also embody or allude to a positive personality or spirit.

Material objects can therefore be said to play a positive psychological (or spiritual) role in our lives when higher, more positive ideals are 'materialised' in them, and so buying and using them daily gives us a chance to get closer to our better selves.

This is not to say that all consumerism just conveniently turns out to be great. It depends on what a given material object stands for. An object can transubstantiate the very worst sides of human nature – greed, callousness, the desire to triumph – as much as it can the best. So we must be careful not to decry or celebrate all material consumption: we have to ensure that the objects we invest in, and tire ourselves and the planet by making, are those that lend most encouragement to our higher, better natures.

Gratitude

The standard habit of the mind is to take careful note of what's not right in our lives and obsess about all that is missing.

But in a new mood, perhaps after a lot of longing and turmoil, we pause and notice some of what has – remarkably – not gone wrong. The house is looking beautiful at the moment. We're in pretty good health, all things considered. The afternoon sun is deeply reassuring. Sometimes the children are kind. Our partner is – at points – very generous. It's been quite mild lately. Yesterday, we were happy all evening. We're quite enjoying our work at the moment.

Gratitude is a mood that grows with age. It is extremely rare to properly delight in flowers or a quiet evening at home, a cup of tea or a walk in the woods when one is under 22. There are so many larger, grander things to be concerned about: romantic love, career fulfilment and political change.

However, it is rare to be left entirely indifferent by smaller things in time. Gradually, almost all our earlier, larger aspirations take a hit, perhaps a very large hit. We encounter some of the intractable problems of intimate relationships. We suffer the gap between our professional hopes and the available realities. We have a chance to observe how slowly and fitfully the world ever alters in a positive direction. We are fully inducted to the extent of human wickedness and folly – and to our own eccentricity, selfishness and madness.

And so, 'little things' start to seem somewhat different; no longer a petty distraction from a mighty destiny, no longer an insult to ambition, but a genuine pleasure amidst a litany of troubles, an invitation to bracket anxieties and keep self-criticism at bay, a small resting place for hope in a sea of disappointment. We appreciate the slice of toast, the friendly encounter, the long, hot bath, the spring morning – and properly keep in mind how much worse it could, and probably will one day, be.

Home

One of the most meaningful activities we are ever engaged in is the creation of a home. Over a number of years, typically with a lot of thought and considerable dedication, we assemble furniture, crockery, pictures, rugs, cushions, vases, sideboards, taps, door handles and so on into a distinctive constellation that we anoint with the word 'home'. As we create our rooms, we engage passionately with culture in a way we seldom do in the supposedly higher realms of museums or galleries. We reflect profoundly on the atmosphere of a picture; we ponder the relationship between colours on a wall; we notice how consequential the angle of the back of a sofa can be and ask carefully what books truly deserve our ongoing attention.

Our homes will not necessarily be the most attractive or sumptuous environments we could spend time in. There are always hotels or public spaces that would be a good deal more impressive. But after we have been travelling a long while, after too many nights in hotel rooms or in the spare rooms of friends, we typically feel a powerful ache to return to our own furnishings – an ache that has little to do with material comfort per se. We need to get home to remember who we are.

Creating a home is frequently such a demanding process because it requires us to find our way to objects that can correctly convey our identities. We may have to go to enormous efforts to track down what we deem to be the 'right' objects for particular functions, rejecting hundreds of alternatives that would, in a material sense, have been perfectly serviceable in the name of those we believe can faithfully communicate the right messages about who we are.

We get fussy because objects are, in their own ways, hugely eloquent. Two chairs that perform much the same physical role can articulate entirely different visions of life. An object feels 'right' when it speaks attractively about qualities that we are drawn to, but don't possess strong enough doses of in our day-to-day lives. The desirable object gives us a more secure hold on values that are present yet fragile in ourselves; it endorses and encourages important themes in us. The smallest things in our homes whisper to us; they offer us encouragement, reminders, consoling thoughts, warnings or correctives, as we make breakfast or do the accounts in the evening.

The quest to build a home is connected with a need to stabilise and organise our complex selves. It's not enough to know who we are in our own minds. We need something more tangible, material and sensuous to pin down the diverse and intermittent aspects of our identities. We need to rely on certain kinds of cutlery, bookshelves, laundry cupboards and armchairs to align us with who we are and who we seek to be. We are not vaunting ourselves; we're trying to gather our identities in one receptacle, preserving ourselves from erosion and dispersal. Home means the place where our soul feels that it has found its proper physical container, where, every day, the objects we live among quietly remind us of our most authentic commitments and loves.

Kintsugi

Kin = golden

tsugi = joinery

The origins of kintsugi are said to date to the Muromachi period, when the Shogun of Japan, Ashikaga Yoshimitsu (1358–1408), broke his favourite tea bowl. Distraught, he sent it to be repaired in China. On its return, he was horrified by the ugly metal staples that had been used to join the broken pieces, and charged his craftsmen with devising a more appropriate solution. What they came up with was a method that didn't disguise the damage but made something honestly artful out of it.

Kintsugi belongs to the Zen ideals of wabi-sabi, which cherishes what is simple, unpretentious and aged – especially if it has a rustic or weathered quality. A story is told of one of the great proponents of wabi-sabi, Sen no Rikyū (1522–1591). On a journey through southern Japan, he was invited to dinner by a host who thought he would be impressed by an elaborate and expensive antique tea jar that he had bought from China. But Rikyū didn't even seem to notice this item and instead spent his time chatting and admiring a branch swaying in the breeze outside. In despair at this lack of interest, once Rikyū had left, the devastated host smashed the jar to pieces and retired to his room. But the other guests more wisely gathered the fragments and stuck them together through kintsugi. When Rikyū next came to visit, the philosopher turned to the repaired jar and, with a knowing smile, exclaimed: 'Now it is magnificent'.

In an age that worships youth, perfection and the new, the art of kintsugi retains a particular wisdom – as applicable to our own lives as to a broken teacup. The care and love expended on the shattered pots should lend us the confidence to respect what is damaged and scarred, vulnerable and imperfect – starting with ourselves and those around us.

Living
Consciously

We want – almost all of us – to live as long as possible. But in our urgent and never-guaranteed search to extend life, we ignore a more realistic and significant possibility: that of altering how intensely we live it.

Crucially, not all time is equal. Time stretches and extends the more we take hold of events, dissect them and turn them over in our minds – just as it seems to shrink and run through us when we only squint at reality, perhaps because we are too scared of the future, sad about the past, obedient to an agenda set by people around us or ambitious about what's to come.

Every minute we are alive is equal from a purely physiological basis, but at the level of the psyche, we can speak of periods of being more or less aware of being here; we can – as it were – live more or less consciously.

Without trying, small children are masters of conscious living – which is why a walk with them to the park may take four times as long as we had anticipated. There are, after all, so many leaves to examine, so many flat large pebbles and so many walls to run one's fingers along.

If time seems to speed up as we get older, it's because we unconsciously decide that we have, in most areas, already noticed everything that it would be significant and charming to see. We walk to the park – and around the globe –

with a blindfold. Our days get emptier because we perceive ever less in them. There is no need to look too closely at trees anymore, or our partner's hands or the cloud formations in mid-afternoon. Matters that would have detained us at the age of 4 lose all definition, until we discover with horror that it is autumn again and we don't know where another year has gone.

The difference between living and living consciously is like the difference between swallowing something at once and chewing it at length. We don't need to be poets or artists to digest our experiences more thoroughly, but we can learn from these disciplines about how to study the world and bottle and preserve its most valuable moments (so that the smell of foxgloves and the song of a thrush will still be alive in us in early February).

We can live more consciously, too, around painful events. Here we can try to slow time's dispersal with a web of questions: what lies behind our fear of people who like us too intensely? Why do we get so irritated by cynicism? Where is this present sadness about work rooted?

Once we master the art of conscious living, we can afford to be a little less concerned with how long our lives will be. Another decade more or less won't have to be the decisive matter when it lies permanently in our power to densify time, and when we can find the amount of content more normally associated with a month in the bounds of a single day. We can slow the reductive march of the clock with the tendrils of our own sensitivity. We should perhaps stop asking how old people are and focus on a more telling and more accurate measure of their time on earth: how consciously they are living.

Melancholy

Melancholy is not rage or bitterness; it is a noble species of sadness that arises when we are open to the fact that life is inherently difficult for everyone and that suffering and disappointment are at the heart of human experience. It is not a disorder that needs to be cured; it is a tender-hearted, calm, dispassionate acknowledgement of how much pain we must all inevitably travel through.

Modern society tends to emphasise buoyancy and cheerfulness. It is impatient with melancholy states, and wishes either to medicalise – and therefore 'solve' – them, or deny their legitimacy altogether.

Melancholy links pain with wisdom and beauty. It springs from a rightful awareness of the tragic structure of every life. In melancholy states, we can understand without fury or sentimentality that no one truly understands anyone else, that loneliness is universal, and that every life has its full measure of shame and sorrow. The melancholy know that many of the things we most want are in tragic conflict: to feel secure, and yet to be free; to have money and yet not to have to be beholden to others; to be in close-knit communities and yet not to be stifled by the expectations and demands of society; to travel and explore the world and yet to put down deep roots; to fulfil the demands of our appetites for food, exploration and sloth – and yet stay thin, sober, faithful and fit.

The wisdom of the melancholy attitude (as opposed to the bitter or angry one) lies in the understanding that we have not been singled out; that our suffering belongs to humanity in general. Melancholy is marked by an impersonal take on suffering. It is filled with pity for the human condition.

There are melancholy landscapes and melancholy pieces of music, melancholy poems and melancholy times of day. In them, we find echoes of our own griefs, returned back to us without some of the personal associations that, when they first struck us, made them particularly agonising.

The task of culture is to turn both rage and its disguised twin, jolliness, into melancholy.

The more melancholy a culture can be, the less its individual members need to be persecuted by their own failures, lost illusions and regrets.

When it can be shared, melancholy is the beginning of friendship.

Monasteries

Today we probably think of monasteries as distant, rather grand and beautiful reminders of the Middle Ages – as far removed from any of the concerns of our modern lives as it is possible to get.

However, in their heyday, monasteries were doing something that retains a universal relevance even for those of a secular disposition. They were highly engineered machines for helping their inhabitants to think. They were begun because certain people wanted to think very carefully about a range of vital questions: what is the nature of God and what does God want from me? What is the divine and what is grace? What is owed to Jesus and what is owed to Caesar?

These believers realised that the human mind is an extremely flighty and easily distracted organ. The prospect of a party at the end of the week, the chatter of a few people out in the street, the sight of an exciting book – all these can derail our attempts to focus our minds.

So, the founders of monasteries went to immense efforts to create environments that could positively assist their members to think fruitfully. They situated their buildings far from cities; they built high walls around their estates; they laid out highly symmetrical gardens and walkways; they made sure their food was nutritious but plain. They encouraged only quiet conversation over meals. They went to bed early and rose at dawn. They did moderate exercise every other day.

Today, we probably don't want to think so much about the particular questions that monks and nuns once focused on. However, we still have a lot of thinking to do. We have equally important thinking tasks to perform around relationships, work and the meaning of our lives.

For these challenges, monasteries retain some important lessons for us. We can be inspired by their ambition to go beyond ordinary expectations and set up ideal conditions where a person might think as well as possible. This contrasts with a more Romantic attitude that sees thinking as mainly influenced by other thoughts – particularly by books – and doesn't quite accept that an organ as elevated as the mind may be assisted by something as ostensibly trivial as going for a walk or having only a light salad for lunch.

In the Utopia, we should learn to design our own highly engineered machines for thinking – institutions geared to the task of deftly extracting our best thoughts from our squeamish and recalcitrant minds.

Moods

Far more than we are inclined to accept and sometimes even realise, we are creatures of mood: that is, our sense of our value as human beings is prone to extraordinary fluctuation. At times, we know how to tolerate ourselves, the future seems benevolent, we can bear who we are in the eyes of others, and we can forgive ourselves for the desperate errors of the past.

And then, at other points, the mood dips and we lament most of what we've ever done, we see ourselves as natural targets for contempt, we feel undeserving, guilty, weak and headed for disaster.

It can be very hard to grasp what causes our moods to shift. A day that started with energy and hope can, by lunchtime, end up mired in self-hatred and tearfulness.

We cannot prevent our moods from being subject to change, but what is open to us all is to learn how to manage the change more effectively – so that our downturns can be gentler, our sadness more containable and our inconstancy less shameful in our own eyes.

Here is some of what we might learn to bear in mind around our capricious moods:

Realise our vulnerability
We should acknowledge how vulnerable our moods are to

being perturbed by so-called 'small things'. We belong to a species of extreme but also fateful sensitivity; we shouldn't expect to be able to appreciate a Mozart aria on the one hand and then, on the other, stay unbothered by the downturned corners of the mouth of a lover. We shouldn't berate ourselves for how thin our skin is; we should adjust ourselves to the full consequences of our extraordinary openness to experience.

Honour the body

Maddeningly, some of why our moods shift is that we inhabit a body. But because it's so humiliating to have to accept that our ideas about ourselves and our lives might be dependent on bodily factors – how long we slept or how much water we've drunk – the temptation can be to insist that our ideas must solely be the offspring of reason. It would be wiser to interpret that most of what passes through our minds is in some way dependent on particular things going on in our bodies.

A small pilot light of kindness

While we are being rocked by a dark mood, we should strive to keep a little light on, the light of sanity and self-kindness that can tell us, even though the hurricane is

insisting otherwise, that we are not appalling, that we have
done nothing unforgivable and that we have a right to be.

This too shall pass
Not only do difficult moods insist that they are correct,
they also seek to convince us that they are permanent. But
our sense of self is naturally viscous; we are condemned to
rise and fall, flow and ebb. Though we may be unable to
shift a mood, we can at least realise that it is only ever such
a thing, and that, in a few hours or days, it too shall pass.

Nature

Nature is valuable not only for itself; it is also to be revered as the single most persuasive and redemptive work of philosophy.

Nature corrects our erroneous, and ultimately very painful, sense that we are essentially free. The idea that we have the freedom to fashion our own destinies as we please has become central to our contemporary worldview: we are encouraged to imagine that we can, with time, create exactly the lives we desire, around our relationships, our work and our existence more generally. This hopeful scenario has been the source of extraordinary and unnecessary suffering.

There are many things we desperately want to avoid, which we will spend huge parts of our lives worrying about and that we will then bitterly resent when they force themselves upon us, nevertheless.

The idea of inevitability is central to the natural world: the deciduous tree has to shed its leaves when the temperature dips in autumn; the river must erode its banks; the cold front will deposit its rain; the tide has to rise and fall. The laws of nature are governed by forces nobody chose, no one can resist, and that brook no exception.

When we contemplate nature (a forest in the autumn, for example, or the reproductive cycle of a salmon), we are witnessing rules that in their broad irresistible structure apply to ourselves as well. We, too, mature, seek to reproduce, age, fall ill and die. We face a litany of other burdens too: we will never be fully understood by others; we will always be burdened by primordial anxiety; we will never fully know what it is like to be someone else; we will invariably fantasise about more than we can have; we will realise that in key ways we cannot be who we want to be.

What we most fear will happen irrespective of our wishes. But when we see frustration as a law of nature, we drain it of some of its sting and bitterness. We recognise that limitations are not in any way unique to us. In awesome, majestic scenes (the life cycle of an elephant; the eruption of a volcano), nature moves us away from our habitual tendency to personalise and rail against our suffering.

A central task of culture should be to remind us that the laws of nature apply to us as well as to trees, clouds and cliff faces. Our goal is to become clearer about where our own tantalisingly powerful, yet always limited agency stops, and where we will be left with no option but to bow to forces infinitely greater than our own.

Philosophical
Meditation

Our minds are filled with out-of-focus feelings and ideas. We dimly experience a host of regrets, envious feelings, hurts, anxieties and resentments. But for the most part, we never stop to analyse or make sense of these. It seems too painful and difficult, because there is always an extra degree of anxiety that attends the process of beginning to think – whatever the eventual benefits.

However, the weight of our unthought thoughts and unfelt feelings can grow unbearable over time. They take their revenge on us for not giving them the attention they deserve. They wake us up in the middle of the night demanding to be heard; they give us twitches and, one day perhaps, serious illnesses. These neglected feelings and thoughts deserve to be examined and unfurled, for they contain a host of clues as to our future direction and needs. They are not merely clutter, as they might seem under a Buddhist lens; they are the jumbled jigsaw pieces of a future, better self.

It is in order to get a handle on the contents of our minds that we require the practice of Philosophical Meditation. Philosophical Meditation proposes that we regularly set aside a portion of time and systematically set ourselves to answer in detail three core questions: What am I currently anxious about that I haven't properly acknowledged? What am I upset or hurt about that I haven't yet fully understood? And what am I currently excited about that I haven't yet clearly identified or had the courage to integrate into my ambitions?

The practice is built on the notion that our brains won't manage to understand their own content without a considerable degree of artifice and training. We need to establish habits that can regularly prompt us to undertake the arduous work of figuring out what is going on in our own minds.

Philosophical Meditation

Phones

Why do we pick up our phones so much? There are the standard, conventional-sounding answers: we check our phones to see if any messages might have come in, if someone posted an interesting video, if something dreadful has happened overseas.

But this is in danger of sounding far too normal and too kind to us. The truth is a lot darker and rather more humbling. We don't pick up our phones to find out what's going on, we pick them up to ensure – with considerable ruthlessness – that we are in no danger of finding out anything more about ourselves.

If we forensically study the moments when we are drawn to pick up our devices, these are almost always when some kind of anxiety is pressing in on us – an anxiety on whose analysis and interpretation the correct navigation of our lives may depend. We are using our devices as an alternative to thinking about our futures, we employ our machines to block insight, to halt the business of processing, to alienate our minds from their most promising and complex substrata.

The thoughts attempting to break into consciousness might be about our mother and the strange thing she said to us over lunch. Or about an unkind and sharp word our partner had with us this morning, which threatens to throw our relationship into question once again.

How convenient that we should have invented a device to ensure that we will never have to meet ourselves again, and how darkly ironic that we should blithely refer to it as, of all things, an instrument of communication.

We take pride in the time we've saved, the dictionaries we don't have to consult, the atlases we can throw away, the many strange and funny things we have discovered. And yet we ignore the reveries we haven't entertained, the ideas we've not hatched, the feelings we've not identified, the self-awareness we've lost.

However, this doesn't need to be the end of the story. Precisely when we most want to pick up our phones, we should learn to do something very unusual; pause and ask ourselves a bold question: if I wasn't allowed to consult my phone right now, what might I need to think about?

The answer can provide us with nothing less than a royal road into our unexamined lives. Rather than using our phones to stop ourselves from thinking, we can study our craving for them as a guide to when and where we particularly need to introspect.

Plan B

We grow up – inevitably – with a strong attachment to a plan A, that is, an idea of how our lives will go and what we need to do to achieve our particular set of well-defined goals. For example, we'll do four years of law school, then move out west, buy a house and start a family. Or, we'll go to medical school for seven years, then go to another country and train in our specialty of interest and hope to retire by 50. Or we'll get married and raise two children with an emphasis on the outdoors and doing good in the world.

But then, for some of us – and at one level all of us – life turns out to have made a few other plans. A sudden injury puts a certain career forever out of reach. A horrible and unexpected bit of office politics blackens our name and forces us out of our professional path. We discover an infidelity or make a small but significant error which changes everything about how crucial others view us.

And so, promptly, we find we have to give up on plan A altogether. The realisation can feel devastating. Sobbing or terrified, we wonder how things could have turned out this way. By what piece of damnation has everything come to this? Who could have predicted that the lively and hopeful child we once were would have to end up in such a forlorn and pitiful situation? We alternately weep and rage at the turn of events.

It is for such moments that we should, even when things appear calm and hopeful, consider one of life's most vital skills: that of developing a plan B.

The first element involves fully acknowledging that we are never cursed for having to make a plan B. Plan As simply do not work out all the time. No one gets through life with all their careful plan As intact. Something unexpected, shocking and abhorrent regularly comes along, not only to us, but to all human beings. We are simply too exposed to accidents, too lacking in information, too frail in our capacities, to avoid some serious avalanches and traps.

The second point is to realise that we are, despite moments of confusion, eminently capable of developing very decent plan Bs. The reason why we often don't trust that we can is that children can't so easily – and we all continue to be influenced by childhood in ways it's hard to recognise. When children's plans go wrong, they can't do much in response: they have to stay at the same school, they can't divorce their parents, they can't move to another country. They're locked in and immobile.

But adults are not at all this way, a glorious fact which we keep needing to refresh in our minds and draw comfort from in anxious moments. We have enormous capacities to act and to adapt. The path ahead may be blocked, but we have notable scope to find other routes through. One door may close, but there truly are many other entrances to try. We do not have only one way through this life, even if – at times – we cling very fervently to a picture of how everything should and must be.

We're a profoundly adaptable species. Perhaps we'll have to leave town forever, maybe we'll have to renounce an occupation we spent a decade nurturing, perhaps it will be impossible to remain with someone in whom we'd invested a lot …

It can feel desperate – until we rediscover our latent plan B muscle. In reality, there would be a possibility to relocate, to start afresh in another domain, to find someone else, to navigate around the disastrous event. There was no one script for us written at our birth, and nor does there need to be only one going forward.

It helps, in flexing our plan B muscles, to acquaint ourselves with the lives of many others who had to throw away plan As and begin anew: the person who thought they'd be married forever, then suddenly weren't – and coped; the person who was renowned in their career, then had to start over in a dramatically different field – and made it.

Amidst these stories, we're liable to find a few people who will tell us, very sincerely, that their plan B ended up, in the end, superior to their plan A. They worked harder for it, they had to dig deeper to find it and it carried less vanity and fear within it.

Crucially, we don't need to know right now what our plan Bs might be. We should simply feel confident that we will, if and when we need to, be able to work them out. We don't need to ruminate on them or anticipate every frustration that might come our way; we should simply feel confident that, were the universe to command it, we would know how to find a very different path.

Premeditation

A premeditation is a technical term, invented by the Stoic philosophers of ancient Greece and Rome, to describe a process, normally to be performed once a day in bed before getting up, whereby one looks into one's future and systematically imagines everything going wrong in it. It is a deliberate, artful, ritualised meditation on varied options for upcoming disasters.

The practice is based on the view that our minds are congenitally unable to face up to the risks we face and do us an enormous disservice through their sentimental, unexamined optimism, leaving us unprepared for the catastrophes that will inevitably come our way. A premeditation constitutes a deliberate attempt to bring our expectations into line with the troubles we face. It builds on a fundamental idea about anger: that we don't get angry simply because something bad has happened; we grow furious only when it is bad and unexpected.

The Stoic philosopher Seneca believed that the greatest service we can pay ourselves is to crush hope. Here is an example of a Senecan premeditation:

The wise will start each day with the thought: fortune gives us nothing which we can really own. Whatever has been built up over years is scattered and dispersed in a single day. No, he who has said 'a day' has granted too long; an hour,

an instant, suffices for the overthrow of empires. Look at your
wrists, a falling tile could cut them. Look at your feet, a paving
stone could render you unable to walk again. We live in the
middle of things that have all been destined to be damaged
and to die. Mortal have you been born, to mortals have you
given birth. Reckon on everything, expect everything.

Of course, premeditation doesn't remove the bad things. But by getting us to admit, frankly and bravely, that we are likely to encounter hell one day, it can leave us a little less distraught when it eventually comes our way.

Ideally, our culture would do some of the work of pre-meditation for us: it would constantly feed us – through a wise emotional education delivered via culture – certain realistic ideas about the sadly demanding and radically imperfect nature of existence. But until it can overcome its congenital sentimentality, we should take care never to start the day without our own private premeditation.

Ritual

Modern culture is very attached to the idea of doing things only once and then moving on to fresh experiences. Novelty and change are centrally prestigious notions; we're eager to explore new places, ideas and opportunities. This attitude comes into particular focus around the status we accord to 'the news', a medium that fundamentally equates novelty with importance.

Correspondingly, we assume there could be nothing more ridiculous than repeating an old idea again and again. Repetition sounds boring and irksome, like the worst experiences of childhood education. But other cultures have taken a different and perhaps wiser view; they have had a high regard for repetition. They have created aesthetically compelling occasions where the same lesson has been rehearsed again and again. Across the globe and through time, it is particularly religions that have been concerned with getting people to repeat ideas. Zen Buddhists have looked at the moon every autumn and written poems in its honour on a set day; Jews will take time to appreciate spring according to a ritual requirement of their holy calendar; Catholics are required to ritually examine their consciences every Sunday; in Russia, orthodox ritual demanded that before a long journey, everyone would meditate briefly on the possibility of never seeing each other again.

What fired the religious devotion to ritual was the realisation that if the goal was to change minds and behaviour (and thereby change the world), once was never going to be enough.

In a secular age, the deep link between religion and ritual has served to cast the very concept of repetition into shadow. This is unfair. In the Utopia, the most important ideas would keep being reinforced via aesthetically compelling rituals. On a regular basis, we would be reminded of the importance of forgiveness, appreciation, self-knowledge and kindness. It's not that we ever actively disagree with such ideas; we simply forget to act upon them in practice. We need rituals to ensure that we properly listen to the significance of all the old things we half-know already, but avoid properly putting into practice, nevertheless.

Simplicity

It can take a very long time indeed to work up the courage to be simple: to read simple books, to wear simple clothes, to have simple days and to say simple things. For a long time, all the advantages and glamour seem to lie with complexity. We are pulled towards rare and hard-to-follow ideas; we entertain our friends with elaborate meals; we pursue convoluted relationships; we have careers that enmesh us in cumbersome commitments; we fill our leisure hours with exotic hobbies.

And then at some point, we may sense and aspire to the real challenge of existence: to dare to sound – to some – like an idiot; to fix on certain basic truths we've always known, to edit down our calendars, to wear only what is comfortable, to put in front of others the same sort of basic foods we like when we're alone, to have relationships solely with those who know how to be direct, to leave our days more or less free apart from one or two elementary pleasures (tending to a garden, having a bath, going for a walk), to limit our reading to books we can understand and to communicate without inhibition all those heartfelt and essential things we know to those we are close to (that they are everything to us and that we'll miss them immensely when it is over).

We worry inordinately about sounding boring or silly were we to show ourselves without elaboration or live according to our own less adorned inclinations. We spend a major part of our lives trying – unsuccessfully – to be somebody else. It can be the thought of death that eventually loosens us from our pretensions. We realise – under its bracing influence – that there is no point burdening ourselves with habits, ideas, vocabularies, people and duties that don't belong to us. There is no point wasting time we can ill afford on those who can't non-defensively say 'I love you', with clothes that we can't keep clean, with books we can't understand and with crowded days heavy with panic and meaningless challenges. We finally lose our terror of coming across as a simpleton.

We'll be properly mature, properly sophisticated even, by the time we learn to appreciate the art of being direct, easy to follow, emotionally straightforward, predictable, unhurried and – in the eyes of the frantic and impressionable many – exceptionally dull.

Small Pleasures

Small pleasures – which comprise such elements as a good night of sleep, a slice of fresh bread or a conversation with a close friend – lack prestige or social support. Our age believes in big pleasures. We have inherited a Romantic suspicion of the ordinary (which is taken to be mediocre, dull and uninspiring) and work with a corresponding assumption that things that are unique, hard to find, exotic, or unfamiliar are naturally fitted to delight us more. We subtly like high prices. If something is cheap or free, it's a little harder to appreciate. We are mostly focused on large schemes that we hope will deliver substantial enjoyment: marriage, career, travel and the purchase of a house.

The approach isn't wholly wrong, but it unwittingly exhibits a vicious and unhelpful bias against the cheap, the easily available, the ordinary, the familiar and the small-scale.

The paradoxical aspect of pleasure is how promiscuous it proves to be. It doesn't neatly collect in the most expensive boutiques. It can refuse to stick with us on grand holidays. It is remarkably vulnerable to emotional trouble, sulks and casual bad moods.

A pleasure may look very minor – eating a fig, whispering in bed in the dark, talking to a grandparent, or scanning through old photos – and yet be anything but.

If properly grasped and elaborated upon, these sorts of activities may be among the most moving and satisfying we can have.

Appreciating what is to hand isn't a defence of failure; it isn't an attack on ambition. But there is no point in chasing the future until and unless we are attuned to the modest moments and things that are available to us already.

The smallness of a pleasure isn't really an assessment of how much it has to offer us: it is a reflection of how many good things the world unfairly neglects. A small pleasure is a great pleasure in waiting; it is a true source of joy that has not yet received the collective acknowledgement it is due.

Sun Worship

In a joking tone, some of us occasionally describe ourselves as 'sun worshippers'. That can mean that we love to tan, visit an island, go to the beach, read a book, sip a drink and perhaps play volleyball. The problem with this approach is not that we are using too grand a term to refer to what is at heart a rather trivial and almost embarrassing enthusiasm; it's that we're arguably making far too little of, and neglecting properly to ritualise or deepen, an orientation that should lie close to the meaning of our lives.

However crowded our beaches may be, in modernity, our love of the sun is for the most part a psychologically shallow and unexplored commitment. Most ancient cultures didn't merely favour a tan, they worshipped the sun in and of itself, regularly bowing before it as the most potent force in the universe, to which they owed gratitude, obedience and adoration. From their sumptuous sun temples spread out along the length of the Nile, the Egyptians paid homage to the deity Ra ('sun'), depicted in their sculpture as a falcon-headed god with a solar disc over his head. The Aztecs incanted sacred poetry to Tonatiuh, the sun god and leader of heaven – while the ancient Celts, under less auspicious skies, expressed piety to Grannus, god both of the sun and, appropriately enough, of wisdom.

Science has taught us enough about the constituents of our distant hydrogen and helium explosion for us not to be able to deify the sun in literal terms. But the star can still occupy a place in our symbolic pantheon, where it may hold pride of place as the supreme emblem of something that no life can subsist for long without: hope.

Most of us have only a tenuous hold on our sources of hope. Despair stalks us relentlessly, especially in the darkness of the early hours. There seem, on many days, so many reasons to give up and surrender to self-loathing. This is why the sun is not merely nice, it is an ally in our mind's constant attempts to structure arguments why it might, after all, be worth keeping going. Maybe there can be an end to the anxiety. Perhaps the project will work out eventually. A lot of things could, in the end, be more or less OK. Such mental explorations the sun seems to reward and generously bolster.

To compensate for our many days of gloom, we should – without any overtly spiritual intent but with a good atheist's appropriate sense of wonder – practise an exercise of bowing down to the sun, closing our lids against its reviving rays, and reciting all the reasons we might still hold on to hope, despite every argument (too often well-rehearsed at night) why we might give up.

The Sublime

The sublime refers to an experience of vastness (of space, age, time) beyond calculation or comprehension – a sense of awe we might feel before an ocean, a glacier, the earth from a plane or a starry sky.

In the presence of the sublime, we are made to feel desperately small. In most of life, a sense of our smallness is experienced as a humiliation – when it happens, for example, at the hands of a professional enemy or a concierge. But the impression of smallness that unfolds in the presence of the sublime has an oddly uplifting and profoundly redemptive effect. We are granted an impression of our complete nullity and insignificance in a grander scheme, which relieves us from an often oppressive sense of the seriousness of all our ambitions and desires and of all our rivals and heroes. We welcome being put back in our place and not having to take ourselves quite so seriously – not least because the agent doing so is as noble and awe-inspiring as a 10,000-year-old ice sheet or a volcano on the surface of Mars.

Things that have up until now been looming in our minds (what's gone wrong with the Seville office, a colleague's cold behaviour, the disagreement about patio furniture) is usefully cut down in size. Local, immediate sorrows are reduced; none of our troubles, disappointments or hopes has very much significance for a time. Everything that happens to us, or that we do, is of no consequence whatever from the point of view of the universe. We are granted a perspective within which our own concerns are mercifully irrelevant.

Bits of our egoism and pride seem less impressive. We may be moved to be more tolerant, less wrapped up in our own concerns. We're reminded of our fragility and transient occupation of the world, which can move us to focus on what's genuinely important, while there is still time. The sublime foregrounds a sense of equality, which we can otherwise find it hard to hold onto. In the face of vast things, the grades of human status lose meaning. The CEO and the intern are equally transient arrangements of atoms.

Our reversals matter less as well. We become more alive to the impersonal, implacable forces that erode all aspects of nature and, hence, all our lives. Like the cliffs under the pressure of the raging oceans, our plans will collapse and fail. Our griefs are universal and unavoidable. The intense burden of the unfairness of existence is reduced.

Crucially, the sublime isn't just an idea; it's a piece of applied philosophy experienced via the senses. The mere idea of our own littleness won't impact upon us just as an abstract proposition. We have to feel it; we have to stand at the edge of the ocean with the wind raging about us or see the Singapore Straits from thirty thousand feet at dawn. The importance of a sensory impression reveals a general truth about how our minds work: pure ideas are feeble tools for affecting human conduct; we can too easily shrug off words. This is why art and travel are ideal resources of culture. At their best, they integrate thought and feeling: the good idea they are seeking to teach us is delivered in the way we need – wrapped up in powerful sensory emotions.

We need not just the idea of cliffs; for philosophy to work its proper effect, we need regularly to take the whole of ourselves out to them.

Unprocessed
Emotion

It is a quirk of our minds that not every emotion we carry is fully acknowledged, understood or even truly felt. There are feelings that exist in an 'unprocessed' form within us. A great many worries may remain disavowed and uninterpreted and manifest themselves as powerful, directionless anxiety. Under their sway, we may feel a compulsive need to remain busy, fear spending any time on our own, or cling to activities that ensure we don't meet what scares us head on (these might include internet pornography, tracking the news or exercising compulsively).

A similar kind of disavowal can go on around hurt. Someone may have abused our trust, made us doubt their kindness or violated our self-esteem, but we are driven to flee a frank recognition of an appalling degree of exposure and vulnerability. The hurt is somewhere inside, but on the surface, we adopt a brittle good cheer (jolliness being sadness that doesn't know itself), we numb ourselves chemically, or else adopt a carefully non-specific tone of cynicism that masks the specific wound that has been inflicted on us.

We pay dearly for our failure to 'process' our feelings. Our minds grow unoriginal from a background apprehension as to their contents. We grow depressed about everything because we cannot be sad about something. We can no longer sleep, insomnia being the outcome of all the many thoughts we have omitted to process in the day.

We need compassion for ourselves. We avoid processing emotions because what we feel is so contrary to our self-image, so threatening to our society's ideas of normality and so at odds with who we would like to be. An atmosphere conducive to processing would be one in which the difficulties of being human were warmly recognised and charitably accepted. We fail to know ourselves not out of laziness or casual neglect, but out of fear and shame.

Processing emotions requires good friends, deft therapists and ritual moments like Philosophical Meditation, in which our normal defences can safely be put aside and unfamiliar material ringfenced for investigation.

The outcome of processing our emotions is always an alleviation in our overall mood. But first we must pay for our self-awareness with a period of mourning in which we gradually acknowledge that, in some area or other, life is simply a lot sadder than we want it to be.

Also available from The School of Life:

Essential Ideas: Love

**From the new pocket book series, featuring key ideas from
The School of Life exploring love.**

The School of Life has distilled its most essential lessons on love in order
to produce a pocket manual that is at once useful and entertaining. We
learn – among other things – how to pick partners more reliably, how to
avoid conflict and how to know whether a relationship is really for us.

We should cease to imagine that a satisfied love life is a chance event;
with this book in hand, it emerges as something that we can all plot for
and achieve.

Love is a skill, not an emotion; this is a guide to how we might master it.

ISBN: 978-1-916753-03-7

Essential Ideas: Self-Awareness

**From the new pocket book series, featuring key ideas from
The School of Life exploring self-awareness.**

Understanding ourselves is the key to unlocking our true potential.

Here is a collection of The School of Life's most penetrating insights
into the puzzles of self-awareness. This book teaches us how to look into
ourselves, how to make sense of our past and how to overcome anxiety
and confusion.

In a highly compressed and entertaining form, The School of Life
introduces us to a person we've been in flight from for too long and will
benefit hugely from getting to know: our deep selves.

ISBN: 978-1-916753-02-0

The School of Life: Calm

The harmony and serenity we crave

A guide to developing the art of finding serenity by understanding the sources of our anxiety and frustrations.

Few life skills are as neglected, yet as important, as the ability to remain calm. Our very worst decisions and interactions are almost invariably the result of a loss of calm – and a descent into anxiety and agitation.

Surprisingly, but very fortunately, our power to remain calm can be rehearsed and improved. We don't have to stay where we are now: our responses to everyday challenges can dramatically alter. We can educate ourselves in the art of keeping calm not through slow breathing or special teas but through thinking. This is a book that patiently unpacks the causes of our greatest stresses and gives us a succession of highly persuasive, beautiful and sometimes dryly comic arguments with which to defend ourselves against panic and fury.

UK ISBN: 978-1-912891-98-6
US ISBN: 978-1-915087-14-0

The School of Life: Small Pleasures

What makes life truly valuable

**Explores and appreciates the small pleasures
found in everyday life.**

So often, we exhaust ourselves and the planet in a search for very large
pleasures, while all around us lies a wealth of small pleasures, which – if
only we paid more attention – could daily bring us solace and joy at little
cost and effort. But we need some encouragement to focus our gaze.

This is a book to guide us to the best of life's small pleasures: everything
from the distinctive delight of holding a child's hand to the enjoyment of
disagreeing with someone or the joy of the evening sky; an intriguing,
evocative mix of small pleasures that will heighten our senses and return
us to the world with new-found excitement and enthusiasm.

UK ISBN: 978-1-915087-03-4
US ISBN: 978-1-915087-16-4

To join The School of Life community and find out more,
scan below:

The School of Life publishes a range of books on essential topics in psychological and emotional life, including relationships, parenting, friendship, careers and fulfilment. The aim is always to help us to understand ourselves better and thereby to grow calmer, less confused and more purposeful. Discover our full range of titles, including books for children, here:

www.theschooloflife.com/books

The School of Life also offers a comprehensive therapy service, which complements, and draws upon, our published works:

www.theschooloflife.com/therapy

THESCHOOLOFLIFE.COM